To Be A Man

To Be A Man

by Robert W. Spike

ASSOCIATION PRESS   •   NEW YORK

To Be A Man

———————

Copyright © 1961 by
National Board of Young Men's Christian Associations

Association Press, 291 Broadway, New York 7, N. Y.

Second Printing, February 1962

Library of Congress catalog card number: 61-14182

Publisher's title stock number: 1468

Printed in the United States of America

For Paul and John

Contents

TO BE A MAN

Preface

Preface

This is a book for people who are asking the question, "What is the style of the Christian life in the mid-twentieth century?"

It is not intended to deal comprehensively with all the intricacies of Christian social ethics, nor is it a treatise on the inner devotional life, although both fields are importantly related to the question.

As contemporary theology has blasted the foundations of a rigid, legalistic moralism that was so widely thought to be the real mark of Protestant Christianity, a vacuum has been left. We have been told with frequency and firmness that abstinence from alcohol, tobacco, and profanity is not the essential mark of the Christian. We are convinced. We have heard stories of men kind and loving to their families who are thieving pirates in business. We agree that such a gap in ethical conduct is far from Christian.

But we are left with little sense of what does constitute the identifiable mark of the Christian man. We need to begin to draw the picture of what that man looks like.

Certainly we are not left without models from which to draw our image. All of us number within our acquaintance men of faithfulness and integrity. Usually these are people who would be embarrassed if anyone suggested that they were models of Christian living. The great reluctance to pin religious labels is in itself one of the most important things that has happened in the days since the decline of moralism as a respectable image.

Nevertheless, in a time when all things are adrift, the man who has begun to set his course in life by Christian teaching about the meaning of life certainly must possess some signs of this loyalty.

The following chapters probe some of the possible consequences of Christian faith in the life of the individual. Christian faith does not begin with a set of maxims for successful living; therefore this is not a book on how to become a Christian.

But since the gospel of Christ is always about God's dealing with men, its communication is very much related to the interaction between theology and practice. The gospel comes alive in any time when men and women begin to alter the course of their natural inclinations in response to it. The gospel is never a private-hearing and self-enfolding experience. Christian faith must be manifested, borne forth as a banner, if it is to be the real thing. The manner in which it is borne forth in daily life influences the whole shape of what Christianity means to an age.

What follows is intended for study and discussion. It is to raise questions that can be pursued with profit for the rest of a lifetime.

The substance of this book was first presented as a series of lectures at the Eighth Triennial Conference of the Association of Secretaries of the Young Men's Christian Associations of North America, in Toronto, May 22-27, 1960. I am grateful for their courtesy and interest.

I am grateful, also, for the help on this book, as in all things related to my work, to Mrs. Robert Poole, secretary and friend.

The Crucial Problem of Response

- *Why is it difficult to describe Christian behavior in personal terms today?*

- *Have Americans lost their sense of destiny and calling?*

- *What is wrong with the traditional way of inspiring people to live a Christian life?*

- *What is the relationship between a belief in God and moral decision?*

- *What does Christ have to do with ethical issues in our times?*

- *Is it necessary to believe in an absolute ethic in order to be a Christian?*

1

The Crucial Problem
of Response

A hundred years ago or more, people knew what
it meant when you said, "He's a Christian gentleman." Now, in most circles, people would suspect
the speaker of being sarcastic about old-fashioned
manners. We tend to believe that the old-fashioned
personal virtues, when practiced ostentatiously,
must be covering some inner weakness. The late
Fred Allen defined a gentleman as "a man who
would not hit a woman with his hat on."

If we are confused about what it means to be a
gentleman, we are even more uncertain what it
means to be a Christian. Emet John Hughes tells
us quite brilliantly what most of us have in mind
as the real standards of manly behavior that we
hold as norms—that which we admire and judge
other men by. He mentions these attributes:

1. He *is* a man.
2. He is a useful man.
3. He respects women.
4. He respects men.
5. He is Himself—and does not try to be a gentleman.
6. He displays special concern for those at his mercy.
7. He listens as well as he talks.
8. He shuns display, as well as discussion of self.
9. He respects conventions.
10. He respects practicalities.[1]

This is a good set of criteria of conduct for a humane and civilized man. To a large extent these attributes are conditioned by the built-in Christian habits of western civilization. And yet, admirable as these traits are, they do not define the Christian man in any dynamic sense.

What goes into the making of a Christian life in these times is one of the genuine puzzles that confront Christendom in these times. There are no easy answers nor neat little prescriptions that can

[1] Emet John Hughes, "The Notion of An American Gentleman," reprinted from *Esquire* (© 1960 by Esquire, Inc.), May, 1960, p. 92.

be passed out like mottoes to be stuck up over our desks.

Two factors are responsible for the great ambiguity that exists when we try to describe the marks of the Christian man.

1. The first is rooted in *the revolutionary changes in the structures of society itself.* In a mass society, dominated by vast impersonal organizations and trends, the personal relationships between men tend to become insignificant and wither in importance. Not long ago America was embarrassed to discover the phenomena of payola and quiz-rigging in its national pleasure ritual, television. This shocked some people, but even more shocking is how many people recognized that this was but a symptom of pervasive changes that have occurred in our sense of what really matters. The pressures of success have quite deadened those feelings of personal honesty that once seemed so important in a close-knit, face-to-face community. William Atwood, in a discerning article entitled "The Age of Payola," probed some of these changes. After extensive interviews with people in all walks of life, from students to housewives, concerning their views on personal honesty, he concluded that "America's changing code of

ethics includes the freedom to chisel." In summary
he also said that Americans are

> under pressure from society to maintain their high
> standard of living. This has resulted in a recasting
> of old standards of right and wrong so that any-
> thing that guarantees success—if you don't stretch
> the law too much—is all right; a deal once con-
> sidered questionable would now be considered
> shrewd.[2]

And perhaps even more important for our consideration, he writes that

> Moral authority has become diffused; the "group"
> is replacing church and family as the arbiter of
> what is done and not done. The group consists of
> others in a community we consider to be like our-
> selves; as such it is incapable of moral direction.[3]

It is one of the amazing sights of our times to
behold a rising tide of secular sociologists, psy-
chologists, and other critics of our culture speaking
in great concern about the destruction of personal
values and calling upon the churches and the
homes to do something about it. In fact, one of the
ironies of our times is to see how much more per-

[2] William Atwood, *Look* Magazine, March 29, 1960, p. 41.
[3] *Ibid.*

ceptive secular critics seem to be about the horrifying implications of much of modern life than the church itself is. The church and the institutions related to her have profited so much by the expansive economy that inside the newly plastered and heavily mortgaged walls, the world doesn't seem so bad.

One of the most eminent, if somewhat maverick, sociologists of this decade, Mr. C. Wright Mills, writes:

> Shaped by an ethos according to which all objects and qualities of life are transient commodities, the [marketing apparatus] would transform the human being into the ultimately saturated man—the [amiable] cheerful robot—and make "anxious obsolescence" the American way of life. There is inherent in this mechanism no social purpose to balance its great social power; no built in responsibility to anybody except to the man who makes the profit. And yet there is little doubt that this mechanism is now a leading fixer of the real values of the overdeveloped society . . . and probably in character building influence—more important than school, the Church, and even the home which it has so intimately involved.[4]

[4] C. Wright Mills, *Social Progress*, October, 1959, p. 10, as quoted in *Christianity and Crisis*, March 7, 1960, p. 22.

So we have a society where the old relationships of personal honesty and trust have little relevance to the larger ethical questions of a mass society.

This fact has suddenly become seriously apparent to the leaders of the nation. During the last part of President Eisenhower's administration, he appointed a Commission on National Goals to try to set down the great overarching values of the nation. A series of crushing blows to national prestige seemed to have driven many to question whether the much professed values of the American life were in effect nothing more than dead tributes to the passions of our ancestors. The Commission itself came up with little that seemed new, nor did it seem honest in its appraisal of what the real drives of American life now are.

John Kennedy owed some of his popular support to the note of challenge to a new dedication for these serious times. With a world afire with new nationalist loyalties, we had seemed to rest back upon complacency and self-congratulation. "Ask not what your country can do for you, but what you can do for your country," he said in his inaugural address. The nation responded, at least for a time, with a sense that this must be indeed a new frontier.

There is real difficulty, however, in appealing to America for a new personal and social austerity. James Reston has pointed out that the new administration was faced with a dilemma. It felt honestly that the Western nations could not prevail in the cold war unless they transformed their societies. On the other hand, the necessity of speeding up our domestic economy called for more spending, and less austerity. This may well be a built-in conflict in the nature of our advanced society.

Added to this is the second factor that makes it difficult to describe Christian behavior.

2. *The theological bankruptcy of what used to be called, in church young people's circles, "personal Christian living."* This was closely tied to a pallid interpretation of the gospel which maintained that it didn't matter what doctrines you held or didn't hold about Christian belief. It only mattered that you followed the teachings of Jesus. The question of which teachings of Jesus—"Love your enemies"; "If any man would come after me, let him deny himself, take up his cross and follow me"; "He who hateth not his mother and father for my sake, is not worthy of me."—was not asked. A man was placed in the impossible position of try-

ing to twist and distort those teachings to fit today's situation, without any feeling of need to do
so. The teachings of Jesus are important only if
one has some special belief about Jesus. Otherwise
the assumption is that simple Christian rules for
living are matters of practical expediency: that is,
ultimately, if you are a good boy, you will feel good,
be happy, and have peace of mind. This is nonsense, as every honest man knows. The teachings
of Jesus do not necessarily lead to happiness, and
as filtered down through nineteenth-century Vic-
torianism, Jesus would be hard pressed to recognize them. One of the most nonsensical statements
in this vein was Mr. Harry Truman's declaration
that the foreign policy of the United States was
built on the Sermon on the Mount. Actually, personal Christian living in this context meant, at the
best, something like Mr. Hughes' definition of an
American gentleman and, at its worst, a kind of
sexless, priggish spirituality bent on repressing all
evil thoughts and the avoidance of offending
people.

The real theological blasts at such a gutless view
of Christianity were fired as reassertions of what
it means for man to be a sinner. People who talked
about Christian living in the old sense were always

offended by such language. To call man a sinner seemed to imply that he wasn't nice enough to do God's work. And such is exactly the truth. Man is everywhere and at all times incapable of pulling himself up by his own goodness to approach unto God. Man is the animal who persistently and with inevitability almost kills that which he loves, grabs before he gives, and wants nothing so much as to work himself out a cozy little world where he can become his own god and rearrange his own universe. Personal Christian living is nowhere to begin an experience with the Living God. You do not begin to try to lay out a design for the Christian life and then work your way along that pattern, gradually discovering how much more like God you are becoming. That was what was wrong with the old concentration on Christian behavior as a primary focus.

The primary experience that men have of God is that He is different from man. He is High. He is Holy. He is Mysterious. He is Awful in imagination and to be feared. Otherwise he is not God; he is a little convenient household idol we have set up so we won't be so scared of the dark. God, the Ancient of Days, our Creator, Redeemer, and Defender, can never be cozied up to. We worship him. We ponder the mystery of his creation and our part in that creation. Religious faith can never *begin* in a concern for practical ethics or it will never get beyond them. It begins as a cry in the night for meaning, as a convulsive yearning for the beyond, the total, my birth and my death in the complex of things.

But then who is Christ? Christ is the answer hurled back across the void in response to our yearning. He is the point of light that has been dug through the opaqueness of our vision by God himself so that we might know where to find Him. In the words of the title of a stimulating recent theology book, he is "The Hinge of History." The Christ event is the key where we begin to find guidance for our understanding of the whole meaning of human history. We do not begin with our little problem of how to manicure our own souls so that we can feel virtuous. We begin with the blast of an ultimate direction and purpose to what, without Him, seems like a crazy and cruel series of accidental events. This is human history. In an age where personal acts seem strangely overshadowed by the massive movement of nations and institutions, we have a gospel which proclaims first of all that Christ is the Alpha and Omega of that history. Nothing could be more distorting of the focus of the Christian gospel than the fundamentalist preoccupation of Christ as *my* personal savior. Of course he is. He is the Lord of all history. And I am a maker of, and a participant in, that history. But to begin and end all religious searching with a neurotic preoccupation as to whether Christ is my personal savior, is to reduce him to the level of being a servitor of the most selfish needs.

The British monarchy is an admirable institution, but the determined way in which every conceivable kind of commercial venture in England gets to be in special appointment to Her Majesty The Queen sometimes seems strange. Once when I was in London, my taxicab nearly collided in Westminster with a massive truck, which turned out to be Such and Such Garbage Disposal Service by special appointment to Her Majesty The Queen. Christianity seems to have a built-in propensity for trying to turn Christ into some such special appointment to our personal whims.

The Christian faith is first of all a freeing from preoccupation with my personal problems, my fears, my doubts, and a being drawn upward toward the vision of God's glorious work in the world. Christ takes up the painfully personal needs and capacities of each man and offers them to God.

"And if I be lifted up, I will draw all men after me." Thus the good news of the Christian gospel is that the far-off and unpredictable God has sent his Son to be with us. And this mysterious event, no matter how you embroider it, or strip it of its mythology and symbolism, makes a fundamental difference in the direction of human life. To be a Christian is to believe the truth of that coming, to confess the truth of Christ's relationship to God, and to respond with joy. The deadness of the church in these times, yes, deadness despite its seeming prosperity, is because even the men inside it do not comprehend the revolutionary implications of that affirmation. They may go on saying creeds and singing hymns, and trying to work out some little niche for religion in their personal lives. But it is all so much nostalgic hogwash if the excitement and unbelievable implications of the confession of Christ as Lord and Savior do not take hold of a man's mind and heart. First of all, in these times the Christian faith demands the disengagement of one's unquestioning loyalties to nation or way of life, even if it be that sacred pseudo-religious shibboleth, democracy. It means straining to understand and to accept one's ultimate loyalty to God's Kingdom. That Kingdom places in judgment all our systems, all our values. Christ's compassion, Christ's justice become for us tokens of what God is really working at in this world, and previews of a glorious consummation of creation. The Resurrection is the sign of that greater resurrection which is to come. This may sound like preacher pie-in-the-sky business to many. And yet this is the doorstep of Christian faith—a radical philosophical and emotional reorientation about the meaning of all human events.

When one sees the gospel as the news of God breaking into human history, of His coming to us without our being worthy or having learned the right combination on our prayer wheel, then personal ethics takes a new perspective. The Christian life becomes a response to that free gift of God. It becomes the new ordering of our life in the light of the new window that has been cut through the blank wall in our life's house. Then a man is ready to think about his personal response to Christ in a new way and to fashion a style of life that is appropriate. Instead of a set of rules that is really Christian legalism, the Christian life is the existential, human response to what Christ seems to be revealing about the nature of the world and of God's action in that world.

Christian ethics change from generation to generation. There is no such thing as an absolute ethic. There are, of course, the time-tested verities of protection for the human community symbolized by the Ten Commandments.

But when one moves beyond these elemental laws of society into the area of how a man or a generation fulfills his or its obedience to Christ, then a whole new dimension emerges. *Ethics* and *ethos* are words that are closely related. Each age produces its own areas of crisis, points where passions are greatest or where the impingement of God's justice is most evident. Each age has its own new wilderness to tame, its own roads to build toward God's kingdom. Sometimes the wilderness wins. Other times a people, or even a single man, makes evident the outline of the Eternal Kingdom in the wilderness of history. That is substantially what the development of Christian ethics is all about. In this mid-century we live in a chromium and plastic jungle where no set of Sunday school maxims bears the slightest resemblance to what Christ demands of a man or a woman. A half-century ago there was a best selling novel called *In His Steps,* in which a Mr. Shelden detailed the account of how a Midwest minister set out to live like Jesus, and what happened to him. The only similarity between that world and this one is that the hero of that book was reviled by his neighbors. Today he would not be, for the things he did; but to try to puzzle out, and to live by, a style that can be called Christian is just as thankless and just as uncertain of attainment in 1960 as in any time. However, the struggle to set down some consensus of what a Christian acts like is terribly important. "By their fruits ye shall know them," says the New Testament. It ought to make a difference, a visible difference, if a man says he belongs to that peculiar tribe of people who have chosen to pin their life to Jesus Christ. It ought not to be, by the same token, a kind of uniform that identifies a man as a member of a special organization who chooses to exercise certain esoteric tastes, or arrogates to himself superior virtue because he bears the stamp of celestial approval. This is always the temptation—to turn faithful obedience into an inflexible armor to shut out the assaults of uncertainty and insecurity that life in this world brings as surely as the dawn—for the Christian as well as the non-Christian.

To be a Christian in any age, and this one is no exception, is to be fully a man—a creature of God, not infallible, not isolated and sterilized by your religion, but responding as a whole being to the times and the people among whom one is set. It means further responding as one who has been freed by Jesus Christ to take a chance, to be experimental, to laugh at fate and cry with compassion, to work and to play: in short, to be a new creature, born of a new birth.

To Be a Man at Work

- *What are some of the major reasons that many people feel frustrated about their work?*

- *Is the increased attention paid to the human relations aspects of industry always a good thing?*

- *Do many people take time to evaluate the real usefulness of their job? Do you?*

- *Are there some jobs that Christians should not do?*

- *Can people with the same kinds of jobs help each other to a better understanding of their work*

- *What would be most useful to you in trying to understand the Christian significance of your work?*

2

To Be a Man
at Work

Ask a man what he "does" and without any
hesitation he knows that you are inquiring about
his job. How a man earns his living, what function
he performs that enables him to be the head of a
household and a member of the community: this
is perhaps the most decisive area in which a man
reveals his basic style of life.

Work patterns have changed radically in the
last few years.

Not long ago I was in an interesting parish in
one of England's most industrial cities. This is a
parish that is well known in world-wide Christian
circles for its daring experimentation in liturgy
and in restoring communication between the
church and the working man. One afternoon a
friend and I were taken on a tour of one of Eng-

land's most distinguished old residences of the nobility. This estate, dating back one thousand years, with its beautiful grounds, had been given to the city and was now preserved intact as a public park. Our guide was a man of about sixty-five, an ex-miner, and member of this particular parish. The vicar had asked him to take us because the man's father had been the head butler under the residency of the last lord.

Fred, our guide, had lived in this estate until he was sixteen. We had a wonderful tour. He knew every part of the house, and the history of all its priceless art and furniture. What is more, in the gardens and grounds he knew routes and vistas that anyone else would have missed. But the remarkable thing was that for the whole of that three-hour tour he never once referred to his having lived there, or to his family's intimate relationship to the place. He escorted us with great dignity, exchanging bits of humor, but with not one word of comment upon his father's role there or his own. It was as if he had completely and absolutely rejected the world in which he had been a part of a tradition of servitude. He remembered that world of order and grace with warmth and appreciation, but it was a world dead and it held no meaning for the present. Over forty years earlier he had chosen a hard, uncertain, and even tumultuous life over a life of gracious and comfortable subservience, and he had no regrets.

This experience with Fred is a parable of the meaning of work in our times—a parable not of the facts, but of the way we try to find the *meaning* of work. There was a time, and really not very long ago, when a man's job fit into a definite pattern of social usefulness. What he did with his hands or performed with his brains, no matter on what level of society, fitted into a scheme of things that he could make some sense of. As a baker he knew the people he was baking bread for, or even as a miner he and his neighbors used coal just like that which he tore from the earth each day. As each year of this century has moved by, man's daily work has gotten further and further removed from a simple relationship to social usefulness. For most of our lifetime we have been hearing warnings about the depersonalization that results for people who have to spend their lives turning a screw on an assembly line in a factory. Now this phenomenon, true once of factory workers only, is more typical of all work than untypical. The world of production in an overdeveloped society is fantastically interrelated. No one creates anything by himself any more, and very few even with the co-operation of a group of people whom they know by name or face. Every industry has auxiliary and supporting industries. Every industry is related to at least one other industry, and that one often is the advertising industry.

My job as a minister in the general service of the church, is one of the last remaining positions of personal involvement and face-to-face satisfactions and evaluations. And yet in working for a large denominational organization I rely heavily on what thousands of local ministers, whose names I do not know, are doing or will do. I depend also very heavily upon the developing co-operative consensus of Protestantism, in effecting changes in thought and program in Protestant churches. I have a sense of performing functions in a wind tunnel, with the work of my hands torn from me and blasted by powerful streams of cultural forces to ends and purposes beyond my control. If this is true of me, what then of someone who works in a plastic toy factory or processes credit cards for the Diner's Club? As our richness as a nation has grown, we have produced a great network of frill industries, conspicuous consumption, and planned obsolescence. Does it not seem amazing that a TV show like *What's My Line?* could keep going for well over a decade, producing two or three fantastic, and often absurd, occupations every week of the year?

It is not true that no one finds any satisfaction in his work any more. That of course is foolish. But we are like Fred. Our work experience is of a different order from that of a generation ago, and yet our explanation of meaning in this work belongs substantially to the past. There are millions of people who are engaged forty hours a week in producing products that hardly contribute to food, clothing, or shelter for anyone. There are millions more whose connection to social usefulness is so remote—a twist of a knob here, a carbon copy filed there—as to seem insignificant.

And yet the lay doctrine of work for the Christian is that work is good because it helps bear the burdens of one's fellow man. Earning money for one's self and one's family is, of course, a powerful incentive for labor, but it has never been able to bear the whole rationale for so important a part of a man's existence as his daily work.

The economists keep telling us that we live in a consumer economy, not a production-oriented one, and we already know it if we are not blind to the flash of multicolored advertisements for every sort of product. Christmas has become the festival, not of Incarnation—the holiness of God become flesh —but the festival of Conspicuous Consumption— the time of admiration for men's cleverness. Last Christmas every luxury gift store featured the ideal gift for Father as an electric drink stirrer. There is no need to weary yourself agitating your scotch and water.

With such a distorted relationship between creation with one's hands and brains and the result of the labor, more and more of our attention is given to the conditions and circumstances under which the work is done. Our relationships with our fellow workers become all-important, and this has mixed results.

If you listen closely to the conversation of homeward bound commuters on an evening bus, you hear how much of the conversation is centered on what a bastard the foreman is, or how ob- noxious Dolores (who sits next to you in the row of thirty-two typing desks) is during coffee breaks. Or, on another level, there is the dreadful preoc- cupation with furnishing denoting status and hierarchy. Only a certain level of executive is entitled to a carpet on the floor of his office and only another level can presume to have a couch, and only the very top has a corner office with a view.

On the better side of this training of attention on the work situation has been the development of a sensitivity to personal relations. Most big companies have extensive personnel departments, and even small employers have been sensitized by the *Reader's Digest* to making employees feel happy in their work—which generally means the boss' trying to act like a human being. Intergroup and human relations problems are the subject matter of extensive university courses. The general philosophy that runs through the courses in one university is referred to as "the p.p.o.v."—the personnel point of view—and by this is meant a collage of psychological and sociological generalizations which aim at viewing each person sympathetically in the midst of his own special environment. Now this is not a bad thing, and there are plenty of work situations that can stand a little "p.p.o.v."

But being humane to your fellow workers is not an adequate vehicle for the Christian response to one's work. To be a man at work, you are compelled to probe the purpose and intent of what you do—the results, if you will, as far as you can understand them.

The Puritan doctrine of work, which rests behind so much of our social thinking, needs to be brought out into the open again. This was a doctrine that made a great deal out of the calling of each individual to some useful work. We generally think of the Puritan New Englander as being obsessed with pious concerns. Our caricature of their concern does not include the fact that they were as interested in the civil calling of a man as in his spiritual involvement. Both orders, they insisted, were ordained by God, and each man had a responsibility in each order. For a man to be lazy in work while pleading that he was wrestling with religious matters seemed to the Puritan fathers as unreligious as neglecting prayer for the sake of work.

Thus the calling of the clergyman was not thought to be essentially any more religious than the calling of a farmer or carpenter.

It is the useful, functional aspect of how a man earns his living that is important. And it must be tied to the most basic understanding of the whole purpose of creation. No man can say he believes

that Christ is the sign of God's purposing work in
history and then step back and say, "I'll spend my
life sitting this one out," or worse, frittering his
life away with petty embellishments and nonsense.
Every man is called to be something by the very
act of what God did in Christ. And how a man
earns his money and uses his creative capacity is
an important part of that calling.

This can be a complicated process in modern
life—the evaluation of both one's own life and the
institutions of modern life, but the fact that it is
complicated doesn't excuse a person from doing it.
There are many factors that go into such an
evaluation. Surely one of the most important is
the conviction that God's purposes for the world
are not necessarily synonymous with all that
western civilization offers in the way of accepted
paths to success. A man really has to challenge the
overwhelming assumption that anything that is
personally profitable and enjoys popular acceptance as a part of the modern economic market is
all right. The drastic antitrust suits of 1961, in
which top executives of two of our most respected
business corporations went to jail because they had
involved their companies in billions of dollars
worth of collusive price-fixing, reminds us of how

great business pressures are. Most of the men involved implied that their activity had been en-
couraged by top-level policy. And even in the professions which seem by tradition and practice to
be obviously humanitarian a man constantly has
to be testing what he is doing by the claims of
Christ. Is the practice of medicine really judged
by the standards of mercy? Does the practice of
law as a man is involved in it steer its course by a
concern for justice? These obvious criteria become
more and more obscured in a commercial economy,
where everything is judged by business standards
of quantitative success. The commercial world
itself must learn the limits of its own freedom in a
world where a wealthy nation like the United
States may be weakened by its own image of
selfishness.

To be a Christian at work is to be first of all a
questioner of the worth of one's work. It is to ask
the worth and the aim and the purpose of a job,
and a whole way of life that is generally unques-
tioned by most people.

If a man is obligated to question the purposes
of a job, two important questions immediately are
framed:

First, doesn't this presuppose a lot more capacity

for abstract thought than the great bulk of the population generally possesses? Probably the average guy doesn't ask himself involved philosophical questions about what it means to be a beer distributor or roofing salesman. But this is where the leadership of the laity in the church is most responsible. It is up to every man with intelligence and leadership ability to be pressing the questions of meaning and to be working toward some consensus within his own vocational groups. Western Germany has pioneered in developing evangelical academies where men from all levels of occupation are gathered to do just this—to probe the meaning of the work realistically and religiously. This is something that a church pamphlet cannot lay out for people. There are no universal prescriptions. Only men sensitized to the gospel, consulting together with their colleagues, can begin to hammer out principles and areas of ethical import for their own vocations. Here and there on this continent small groups of men are meeting to do this—lawyers, small business men, doctors, accountants, and many others. This is such a complicated economic system we inhabit that a vast uncharted wilderness waits before laymen at this point. Broad injunctions to treat people kindly and not to cheat are not adequate. We need depth analysis by people who themselves are involved before we will even know what the issues are— around which ethical decisions can be made.

A second question is: Will not many people find out, after they are heavily involved in a way of life, that they ought to get out of it?

The first answer to this is an unequivocal "yes." Many already have found out. There is such questioning that one church agency has set up a special office to deal with men who, awakening suddenly to the demands upon their lives for significant occupation, need help in locating it. This office does not intend to get these men jobs primarily in church positions. Quite the contrary, it will help them get jobs in places where they are needed for their skills as men and craftsmen. For example, a new town in North Dakota, where a large settlement of Indians just off the reservation have located, desperately needs an industry to be the economic base for the community. These people could start a canning factory of local products if they had someone to merchandise the products. Here is an ideal job for a man with wholesale merchandising experience. It would mean a drastic salary cut, but that might be a part of finding one's self vocationally in this culture. To suggest that the Christian life can be followed painlessly or that what is being talked about is developing a new harmonious integration of personality is to miss the point.

One has to face the fact frankly that many jobs are meaningless, and a man has two choices he can make when he honestly faces that fact. He can leave—pick up his tent and his family and take a long deep breath and go elsewhere. Or he can grit his teeth, earn his pay check, and begin to fulfill his real calling in the time outside the job.

This moves us to another consideration. In the mid-twentieth century on this continent it is not sufficient to think of a man's work as being confined to that for which he gets paid. It is really necessary for us to stop thinking of two categories, work and leisure time. A man's true responsible involvement in the world transcends his payroll listing. He has far more time outside of the office than he ever had. What is more, our society is an intricate intermingling of political and economic institutions, and despite the oratory of business leaders or politicians, neither the modified capitalism nor the modified democracy under which we really live could exist apart from the other. Therefore a man's real work may be in local politics, serving on the school board, or even acting as a writer of letters to the editor—a self-appointed guardian of public right.

The Christian's vocational calling in this time— to be a man in stubborn response to what he thinks God intends for men rather than what the society seems to allow—ought to be expressed in a great variety of ways.

A lawyer with good connections in a well-known firm may decide to go into politics, risking his future for the adventure of responsible government, or he may decide to devote a certain part of his practice to the more adequate defense of people without connections and funds, or even righteousness, on their side.

A salesman of some new household gadget may decide to keep at it, but to try to measure his sales claims and promotion schemes by rigorous standards of truth, or he may decide that his calling as a salesman ought to be related to something more vitally related to human need.

A public utility worker may take pride in his work and find additional usefulness helping to organize a non-unionized group of employees, or working toward the improvement of an existing employees' organization.

A doctor, whose work is so very obviously a holy calling, may take a new look at the quality of his work, or begin to examine the policies and practices of the local medical society and perhaps of the American Medical Association.

These things do happen, and with increasing frequency. The individuality and variety of each response is an important consideration. But this is not enough. Not every man has enough imagination to put together a theology of Christian history and its implications for "me" in my work. Vocational groups need to gather to hammer out in greater detail the ethical issues involved in ever more complex constellations of professions, and more than that to spell out more explicitly the "theologies of callings." And there are ways of earning a living besides robbery and peddling narcotics that are certainly immoral. There was a time when liquor dealers were separated out for this dubious category. Most of us no longer believe that it is an inflexibly evil business as compared to businesses of mass destruction, or perhaps mass narcotization.

The development of black-listed professions

would be a bad thing. So would the development
of "how to be Christian though engaged in a useless profession" kits. But we do need a great deal
more writing that takes seriously the new orders
of our society with authentic detail and wisdom.
We need to accompany the extensive vocational
guidance programs of high schools with a Christian conception of work and calling that is more
than pious generalities.

The Evangelical Academies in Germany have
been gathering laymen together ever since the
war to discuss their work and their vocation. In
this country there are many places where such
programs are being carried on. The Austin Ex-
periment in Austin, Texas; Parishfield, Michigan;
and Packard Manse, Stoughton, Massachusetts,
are only a few such places.

For a decade American churches have talked
about vocational ministries. There are nowhere
nearly enough such enterprises now going on.

This kind of program is as crucial as the development of theological seminaries for ministers,
and we ought to get on with it.

To Be a Man at Leisure

- *Who has the most leisure today?*

- *Why don't more people enjoy their free time?*

- *Is there any standard you can apply to measure the most meaningful ways to employ your leisure?*

- *Is it snobbish to be concerned about good taste?*

- *How can you find time to have quiet meditation?*

3

To Be a Man
at Leisure

The work life of America has to be seen increasingly against a backdrop of a life of play and amusement.

Love Field, Dallas, Texas, has an enormous new airport terminal building. In addition to elaborate public accommodations, it has a number of shops which feature a larger number than usual of gifts, toys, and flashy thingamabobs. On a long six-hour layover there I decided to buy some inexpensive gifts for my sons. There was really almost nothing that fit this adjective, although there probably has never been a larger collection of amusing and diverting trifles. One gizmo was particularly interesting. It was a toy radiometer. Enclosed inside a clear plastic case were two whirling blades which rotated when exposed to bright light. It was breathlessly described by the publicity blurb as a Light Motor—an amazing scientific toy. For the small sum of $2.00 your child could watch these blades whirl. But this amazing motor could be harnessed to no purpose. It just churned madly when exposed to light. Some children might be sent into ecstasy over this scientific wonder, but most, I'm sure, would say "So what!" This toy is a good symbol of the empty motion of much of our life. We have harnessed the secrets of natural power and embellished them and magnified them, and then often set these powers to turning bright-colored, impotent windmills.

Dr. David Barry, writing about the tragedy of what goes out over many TV channels, asks, "Does it not seem sinful to tame the secrets of electronic power and then harness them to an amusement park?"

Never before in history has a nation possessed so much time freed from the necessity of labor, and yet one of the constant physical complaints, that doctors hear most frequently, is, "I feel tired all the time." The amount of leisure time, however, is not spread evenly across the class spectrum. There are parts of the world where people still work long hours six days a week, even on this continent. Unionized industrial workers have become accustomed to the forty-hour week or less, and every indication is that the standard measuring unit will become a four-day work week within the near future. The automation revolution makes this inevitable. One of the ironies of leisure in this culture, however, is that as it has increased for the worker, it has often shrunk for the manager and executive. With no union set scale, he often throws himself into the pursuit of the competitive market with a reckless disregard for his own health. He moves at such a fast pace that on an average Friday night, while his employees may be heading for the nearest lake to fish, he may still be standing first on one foot and then the other waiting on the standby list at Midway airport boarding gate wondering if he will get home to New York tonight. So when he does get a moment's leisure, he pursues it with the same mad speed as his business, in effect trying to catch up, by compulsive recreation, with the time he has missed.

There are two conflicting motifs that characterize American leisure time: first, a great sense of vacuity, of time emptied of meaningful activity; and second, an impression of determined frenzy to relax, to unwind, to do something different.

These two moods are related; the variegated skein of leisure activities seems designed, in the main, to divert from facing the emptiness. Recreation, entertainment, and leisure enterprises are big business in the United States. When you think of the whole gamut of interests that run from pinball machines through books, magazines, TV, sports equipment, and on to serious cultural offerings like theatre and music, you realize that a very high percentage of our national consumer expenditure is related to the use we make of our free time. The most expensive kind of advertising of consumer goods is related to the entertainment industry, namely, commercial television.

It is almost impossible to assess the value and influence of so varied a field as leisure-time offerings in this country. We all are aware of the grandeur of what is now available to the commonest man in the way of music, art, drama, and literature. But we are even more aware of the junk, the time wasters, the trash, and on an even greater scale, the just plain expendable forms of entertainment that are offered.

Alberto Moravia writes of American magazines,

Restful reading these American weeklies. . . . Le Corbusier said that the modern house should be a machine for living. But the Americans have gone him one better; they have invented a machine for reading without ruffling the surface of your mind.[1]

It is this prevailing quality that causes the most alarm about our leisure, and causes one to ask the question, "What does it mean as a Christian man to be freed from labor for so great a portion of his time?" Such a question raises some little resistance in all of us. No one wants to be told how to spend his free time. "Exhort me about my Christian responsibility in my work, if you feel compelled to, or implore some moments for church work, but keep your hands off my recreation—you kill-joy!"

But fundamental to the Christian affirmation is that Christ is the sovereign of all of life, that there is no area from which he can be barred or in which he does not feel at home. We have heard this, or some variant thereof, many times and generally as a springboard for exhortations to behave ourselves, or warnings against strong drink or shady and indecent amusement. This is not the most pertinent leap that should be made. There are four considerations that a Christian should make as he evaluates his leisure time:

[1] Alberto Moravia, "The American in Italy," *Esquire*, February, 1960, p. 48.

1. The first is that, as far as the calling of the Christian is concerned, the distinction between work time and leisure time is a false one. A man's job may be so meaningless that the only way he can relate himself to God's creating and redeeming purposes is through efforts made after work. And even if the job itself is productive, modern specialization may make it so restricted in scope, if not in importance, that a man must take on some other responsibilities or avail himself of opportunities in order to be fully a man, co-worker with God in the world's redemptive life.

Jean Genet, a Frenchman, has written a fascinating play called, *The Balcony*. It is a savage satire on the overwhelming need of modern man to escape from his technological strait jacket by playing roles. The whole play is set in a fantastic house of prostitution during a revolution in some unnamed European country. The ingenious madam has arranged thirty-eight different studios, each furnished to portray some fantasy that her patrons may wish to indulge in during their visit. There are extensive props and costumes, so that a man may assume the role of a general, a judge, or an archbishop as a part of his sexual escape from reality. In the second act the revolution is successful. All the responsible officials of the country are wiped out save the chief of police of this capital city where the house is located. He also happens to be the patron and protector of the fancy house, and as he comes into power, he makes the madam the queen of the country. All the people caught in their roles of fantasy in the house of prostitution have to assume the real roles. Thus a poor clerk becomes Archbishop, and other rather depraved souls Judge and General, and so forth. It is really a savage play in which reality and role-playing become so intertwined that one cannot be told from the other. And at the very end, the madam addresses the audience as she leaves, "You must now go home, where everything —you can be quite sure—will be even falser than here." There is no one present who does not ache a little from the knowledge of his own hypocrisy.

And yet there is a constructive side to this dividing up of a man's life that is so typical of our times. He can use this ability given him by speed and money to hide continually from himself in an ever diminishing mirror act, like Alice stepping through the looking glass, and yet another glass, and another, and another. Or he can in a sense multiply his energies and his gifts to become a more useful human being. He must be aware, however, of who he is, a child of God, subject to all the temptations to begin acting like a little god with his multiplication of power and resources. Even the most devoted community leader may use his activities to hide the fact of his own mortality from himself, and to begin to act like an institutional ad for the Most Distinguished Citizen rather than like a human being. The importance of self-awareness for the Christian cannot be over-emphasized. This does not mean that every one of us has to go through psychoanalysis, although more people in positions of responsibility and complex social responsibilities would benefit by it, in a time when all role shapes and meanings are changing. It does mean, though, that the development of rigorous self-criticism, a sense of humor, the ability to use power without arrogance, or of meeting aggression without being pulverized on the inside—are all things that a man needs if he will live a fast life, moving from job to avocation and to play without tearing himself apart. And it may very well be, to turn the irony of *The Balcony* back upon itself, that a man's role-playing as a part-time hobbyist or community leader may be the most important part of his calling. Do you remember the "thinking man's filter" ads? These supercilious spots capitalized on the unusual contrast between a man's job and his avocation. For a Christian, the holding of time together in a bundle of important interests is not such a silly thing as the cigarette boys made it out.

2. The second thing to be lifted up is a stress on one particular use of leisure time as an extension of a man's vocation. That is, his job as a participating citizen in this democracy. One of the disturbing things about our rich economy is that we almost starve our public services while we pad our private nests. Only a few towns or cities in our countries have really adequate schools, libraries, recreational facilities, health services, in comparison to the lushness with which we have endowed our private clubs and our own homes. We have been misled by cries of "socialism" into glorifying self-indulgence. The intractable and old-fashioned attitudes of the American Medical Association on public health policies are a shameful illustration of disregard for the body politic. It is a struggle everywhere to get continuous support for voluntary community agencies. There are so many worthwhile agencies, public, quasi-public, and private, that need the support, both fi-

nancial and personal, of the men of the community. As diseases get more and more organized, and as public services get more and more expensive, it is going to be even more difficult to get people to work faithfully as volunteers.

And yet we need citizen involvement far beyond these public services. The need for more astute politicians in every community is a pressing one. We all bemoan the ineptness *and* the weakness of party politicians and candidates, yet few are willing really to get involved. Much of this results from a misunderstanding of the political process. We think compromise dirty and vulgar in the public realm, although we are often willing to practice the same art in our business. It is really on the level of precinct workers and local candidates that more men of conviction need to act. This usually cannot be done on a one-shot "reform" type ticket, which nearly always carries with it the seeds of its own failure even if successful in a single enterprise. Only those who really involve themselves in the political process, club membership and all, really can carry through in most instances. There are of course times for extreme, insurgent actions, or else the political parties become completely enmeshed in their own self-interest. Most Protestant morality crusades completely miss this point. The needs and the issues of responsible government are on a far deeper level. Some years ago I was deeply involved with a small group of political amateurs, who because of their hard work in a presidential campaign found themselves in a position to wield real power in local politics. The only trouble was that there was no one in the group who felt able to give himself completely to the job of being a candidate behind which the group could mobilize. There were many good intentions and ideas but no one really willing to pay the price of invasion of privacy, personal abuse, and just plain hard knocks that the front man would have to take.

Beyond political citizen responsibility there is another kind of use of leisure that the Christian man ought to take seriously. That is involvement in front-line unpopular causes. The past decade in the United States has been one in which people tried to hide behind one another and blur into the crowd. There are signs that this is not so true as it once was. The time is overripe for the kind of student action that has accompanied the Negro sit-in demonstrations. They have been instructing their elders. The individual in a supine and voiceless public must find his voice and give his time and energies to focus public attention on the real issues of our times.

For example, as important as P.T.A. may seem to be to the school, one rarely attends a meeting without thinking of the superficial issues it usually is concerned with. There are many other clubs and organizations in most communities that have even less vital issues confronting them.

Reinhold Niebuhr has said that our land is now a "gadget-filled paradise suspended in a hell of international insecurity." We must not waste our time in dealing with obvious things for the sake of good community feeling. The Christian layman is called to be a disturber of the peace on issues that confront the human race. Injustice and agony bedevil this world, and in such a world he must take his stand in unpopular places.

3. The third observation is in quite a different mood. Christians keep needing the reminder that God's creation is good and we can enjoy it. It is amazing, with all the options for choosing activities, how few people seem really to enjoy themselves these days. The superficial impression one might get on a summer Saturday is that the land is indulging in a hedonistic holiday of speed boats,

camping, golfing, picnicking, and travel. But just below the surface one senses a kind of oppression of accoutrements. Have you ever camped in a national park and beheld the load of supplies that people are cluttered with, as they supposedly are going back to nature for a bit? It is certainly not a universal description, but there is a certain amount of joylessness in our amusement. It seems to be compounded of two ingredients—first, a deeply buried hangover from our Puritan past which makes us feel guilty about enjoyment, fun, and a deep savoring of sensation; and second, the pile of gadgets which burden rather than free.

Our culture is often accused of being too material. It may be, in the sense that we have so much of everything that we get our feet stuck in it. But in another sense we aren't material enough. We let things use us. We need to be more at home with the physical and the earthy. We are becoming too cerebral and abstract a race. We need, in our leisure, the experience both of enjoying physical activity and of learning the processes of discrimination as to what really feeds the inner needs of taste and enjoyment if we are to be human. We need to enter into this material life as its master and not as its slave. This means both the development of the body and also the development of artistic appreciation. This does not mean self-conscious, arty phoniness, but the almost instinctive knowledge of what is truly creative, what speaks truth in beauty or in vividness. This takes exposure to good art, to exciting theatre and music. Too many men either ignore these fields or, if they take one of them up, do so as if it were an assignment or a medicine. The subtleties of color and of sound in true art have a deeply healing quality that we need. They are not esoteric, but as truly physical as swimming or golf.

4. The last observation on the Christian man at leisure has to do with an extension of this joying before the Lord in his creation. It is the need for reflection and contemplation. No one can know who he is before God and his fellow men if he is running breathlessly all the time. The disciplines of silence and quiet are the rarest experiences in a loud world. Even public conveyances and their terminals feel they have to fill the air with canned music to keep people from facing themselves. There is always some kind of barrier, either noise or color, to keep us diverted from looking inward and listening to the cries of our unspoken and half-finished thoughts.

We are starved for thoughtfulness in this time. We are in need of inner strength that comes only through quiet reflection. A man who does not take stock of himself in all candor, or who does not allow time for the creative processes of association and relationship to bubble up through his consciousness, is only half a man. This may take many different forms. More and more men actually spend one day a month in a retreat house. Others stay home or go off by themselves to the sea or the woods. It can happen in a hotel room where no one has your phone number. To be a man, a full man, in the complexity of our life is to find a rhythm for your life, alternating between deep, courageous, intelligent engagement with the world's needs, and times to evaluate, relax, and lie back in complete trust upon the everlasting arms of an all-sufficient God.

To Be a Man in Love

- *Is "love" a goal toward which people strive or is it an unpredictable gift?*

- *Are the traditional roles of man and woman in our society changing for the worse?*

- *Do we worship youth?*

- *What constitutes pornography?*

- *Is sex sinful?*

- *Is there any relationship between the love of God and the love of men and women?*

4

To Be a Man
in Love

The text might be taken from James Thurber, one of the wise men of our day. Discussing the subject of love in the United States, he says, "My pet antipathy is the bright detergent voice of the average American singer, male and female, yelling or crooning in cheap yammer songs of the day about 'love.' Americans are brought up without being able to tell love from sex love, Snow White or Ever After. We think it is a push button solution, or instant cure for discontent and a sure road to happiness, whatever it is. By our sentimental ignorance we encourage marriage as a kind of transquilizing drug. A lady of 47 who has been married 27 years and has 6 children knows what love really is and once described it for me like this: 'Love is what you've been through with somebody.' "

This, in capsule form, is a profound truth which might describe the response of the Christian man in the whole never-never land of sex, lust, marriage and the family, and love. We use this word in so many different ways to mean so many different things. Love in one context is a word for the purest and most ethereal of feelings. It is an exaggerated form of casual liking when we sign it to a letter. It is also sometimes a synonym for sexual intercourse whatever the quality of the relationship, just another four-letter word. It is no wonder that we are confused about male and female and about what it means to be man and woman in our culture.

There are at least four factors that contribute to our confusion, and they are so interrelated that it is almost impossible to assess cause and effect. There is the greatly changed role of women in our society and the consequent upheaval in what normative masculine and feminine behavior is thought to be. There is the cult of worship of youth and adolescence in our society. There is the preoccupation with public sex symbols and the conscious commercial manipulation of these symbols. And underneath there is the residue of guilt and shame that post-Calvinist Protestantism and Irish Catholicism fastened upon us.

Let me amplify a little bit on each of these factors.

There is not much need to document the fact that women in our society have, in half a century, found new freedom and a new sense of partnership in all areas of modern life. It is also true, as any honest and thoughtful modern woman will tell you, that there is as much pain and uneasiness derivative from this new freedom as satisfaction. The inner war between the primary, aggressive, action-taking role in society and the need to be protected, sought after, and, indeed, hidden from primary action is a real one for the woman. And a man feels a tremendous sense of deprivation, almost of surgery, in having taken from him the hidden reserve of the dutiful and waiting wife. There is no way back from this great transition, nor should there be. But in a society where the roles of men and women have begun to look more alike, there will be a blunting of what was thought to be purely feminine and what was thought to be purely masculine behavior. This is very threatening in its result to many people and seems to shake the very foundations of being. It means quite frankly a real shift in sexual customs, and no amount of hand-wringing will change this. It means that there will be a greater amount of experimentation. Such a time of discovering new balance of responsibility and role for male and female behavior is bound to be a time of explosiveness and, indeed, of personal tragedy. For one thing, it is inevitable that overt homosexuality should be increasingly a problem.

Now the second factor—what can be called the cult of youth worship—may need some explanation. Perhaps there has not been a time in history when adolescence was such a preoccupation as it is today. Everything from mass advertising to public institutions are affected by this preoccupation. In a way, those who are concerned about youth are glad to see such attention paid to this important part of our population, but we need to be alarmed by the way in which adolescence is made a mystique and the arbiter of taste and culture. The fear of juvenile delinquency, for example, has become one of the real obstacles to communication with teen-agers. They have been walled off by this image of the psychical violent young animal which the public has somehow thrown around them. Policemen in overly-protected suburban communities act as if a juvenile crime wave had erupted out every time a good honest fight breaks out between a couple of boys on a street corner. This fixation on adolescence, a compound of attraction and fear, may have something to do with the artificial way our times treat death. Donald Soper, the great Methodist outdoor preacher, in the Beecher Lectures at Yale in 1960, pointed out some of the differences preachers find in their audiences as distinguished from fifty years ago. One of the greatest, he said, is that death expectancy has been pushed off twenty-five years or more for the majority of people listening. This has a profound psychological effect on people in many ways. They are not obliged to come directly to terms with their mortality in the midst of their common life. Mother and father, and even grandpa and grandma, stay close by a lot longer. When life can become so much the sole conscious concern of a people, they begin all the more to hate and fear death and to repress this awareness as deeply as possible. The dream of eternal adolescence is placed in the center of consciousness, and the unrelieved fear of death is pushed ever more deeply into the unconscious.

This fact may also have something to do with the third factor of sexual ambiguity mentioned in the beginning—the enormous public display of sexual symbols. Visitors to North America are often shocked by our glamorized, larger-than-life display of these symbols. They are not shocked by honest expressions of sexual feeling but by the breast-and-leg cult, the vulgar, suggestive, almost leering attitudes so much of our commercial advertising displays. We are so barraged by it, all the way from ads for movies to television commercials for cigarettes, that to a certain extent we don't pay much attention to it consciously any more. But the motivation research people who guide and advise commercial advertising follow Freudian clues with a fixed and determined purpose. No association or double entendre is accidental, you can be sure. These men know with precision the adolescent fantasy life of Americans, and they exploit it to sell things with enormous success.

There are those who are very concerned about sex and violence in the movies. Most of the new movies that have been attacked do deal very directly and realistically with sex in the context of contemporary experience. Perhaps there is some good in this. It is the masquerading and draping of sex in religious spectaculars, the prurient voyeurism that seems to say that any unfulfilled suggestiveness is all right as long as conventional morality triumphs in the end and only the imagination is tantalized, that is disquieting. Al Morgan, former TV executive and now a novelist who writes social criticism, said recently on this subject (perhaps with some exaggeration) that the *Ladies Home Journal* was one of the most pornographic magazines in America, and that he wouldn't mind his children seeing *Room at the Top*, but he had forbidden them to see *The Ten Commandments*. The indulgence in sexual thrill under the guise either of earnest objectivity or religious frenzy is what he objects to.

Underneath all the blatant sexuality of our public images there is an underground river of fear and guilt, that can be traced at least in part to our early Puritan fear of excesses, the austere and disciplined code of our spiritual forefathers, stained and discolored by the Victorian sense of romantic tragedy. This lingers with us. And despite our outer guise of emancipation, we still have a feeling that sex is dangerous, perhaps even unclean.

In the foregoing description there are some

hints of what the stance of the Christian man in love ought to be, but they need to be spelled out even more precisely. If it is true that we live in a time when the roles of men and women are changing, that we unduly emphasize adolescence, that we are a public of peeping toms as far as sex symbols are concerned, and that underneath there is a hidden river of fear and disgust, what does it mean to be fully a man in such a time?

First, the Christian man believes that the body is good and a part of God's providential creation. Most of us would acknowledge this individually, but the church as an institution does not often seem to be fully committed to the idea. Halford Luccock once told a story about

> the woman who had been involved in a minor accident (and) was closely questioned about how it happened. Asked if her brake was on, she replied with some heat that she was careful always to drive with the emergency brake on, so that in case an emergency arose she would be ready.[1]

Now, institutional and official Christianity has often acted like this about sex. It was afraid to

[1] Halford Luccock, reprinted by permission from *The Christian Century* (copyright 1960 Christian Century Foundation), May 18, 1960, p. 623.

speak very positively about the goodness of the flesh, for fear people would gallop off with this gospel to a wild sensuality. So the emergency brake is always on. And despite the great increase in instruction about sex, the most positive attitude one seems to encounter as a result is that the body is a kind of neutral blob of protoplasm, but with a kind of predisposition to get people into a miasma of trouble. This is not the biblical view seen in large perspective. William Cole's book, *Sex and Love in the Bible*,[2] seems overwhelmingly to indicate that the physical, and the sexual, is not just neutral, awaiting some spiritual infusement, but a good and wonderful part of creation to be enjoyed. This does not mean that a man can't use his body sinfully. He can, in the same way that he can use his mind and his deeds. He can use sexual aggression and exploitation in cruel purposes. But sexual appetite and desire are not per se the seat of selfish sinfulness more than any other part of the human appetites. Indeed, contemporary psychoanalytic knowledge reveals to us how profound was Jesus' remark that "he who lusteth after a woman in his heart hath already committed adultery with her." That is, the close, indissoluble

[2] New York: Association Press, 1959.

union between all parts of the human personality is such that a man who has a compulsive pattern of promiscuity and a man who treats all women who work for him like dirt may be brothers under the skin.

The Christian man thanks God for his sexuality, teaches his children the same thankfulness, and shows mercy and forgiveness to those around him who are caught in the bondage of sex fascination.

The second consideration he needs to have before him is that sex is not magic. There is a vast difference between the honest acceptance of the sexual dimension to life and the glamorized confusion that it is the answer to all possible problems. Russian attitudes on sex, marriage, and divorce are revealing to us. Little attention, in comparison to us, is given to the whole matter of sex and love. Nudity in art is frowned on, and any attention to the physical side of love is omitted. Remember Mr. Khrushchev and "Can Can"? Romantic love is discussed by young people on a high spiritual plane, much like the Victorian period of our own society. Social work knows practically nothing of the case histories of sexual pathology that we know.

What are the reasons? Some of them are not

good. It is a part of the unnatural, static idealism of a philosophy which turns its back on everything that is not rationalistic. Another reason, though, is that the social goals of the people, however wrong, are the real driving motivations. Preoccupation with sex as personal fulfillment is just not needed. Now for us, the degree to which we worship the Hollywood variety of sexual romantic love is a measure of our own loss of overriding religious and ideological purpose. All else having failed us, cynical of the purposes of history, with God as an irrelevant superstition, we cling to romantic love as the one magic talisman.

There is an excellent novel called *The Optimist*, by Herbert Gold. It is one of the most discerning pictures of how desperately love becomes the only real worship center of many Americans and how this is not enough. Late in the book, the hero, Burr Fuller, a bright young lawyer with a political future, and his wife, Laura, his college sweetheart, find there is nothing left in this particular shrine for them. Here is an excerpt describing their unhappiness:

> Burr forced a wedge into the long summer evening. They were trying. They were spending the evening together. He put on a Segovia record while

Laura showered after they both tucked the boys in bed. He tapped on the door and told her he was just taking a stroll around the block, right back. Like all Americans, Burr made much of sex. He made love of sex, either in Puritan denial or Protestant expectation, as if the hard, little burning light focused through the magnifying glass were really the whole of the sun. Yes, it is that light; it does burn mightily and it can distract from the immense timeless daylight giving power of the unseen sun.[3]

Sex is not magic. It is sacred because it is a part of God's mysterious creative process, but it is not to be tamed to achieve Nirvana.

The last point is that, for the Christian, love is the gift of response. Isn't it interesting how the Bible is always using the marriage relationship as an analogy of God's relationship to His people? This analogy can work both ways. God's relationship to mankind, his love for us, tells us also something about what earthly love is like. In the biblical view, God takes a terrific chance, a daring step into the midst of his creation and makes a covenant with his people, and though men break the trust and betray the confidence, God never

[3] Herbert Gold, *The Optimist* (Boston: Little, Brown & Co., 1959), p. 336.

leaves. He is long-suffering. He is beyond the darts of contempt and the weapon of hatred. He is Christ on the cross. That is the nature of his love, and our love is given out of our response to his faithfulness, his daring act in our history. And so it is with real human love. It is kindled perhaps in the excitement and awakening of two people daring to reach out to each other in sexual attractiveness. But it burns steadily only in covenant, in continued response to one another in full depth, in family life, through the valleys and up the peaks. As the woman said to James Thurber, "Love is what you've been through with someone."

The Bible never could have used love and the marriage relationship as an analogy of God's relationship to us if the present Hollywood view of this had been current. Take the Hollywood biblical spectacular called "The Story of Ruth." In one way they do rather well in depicting the main point of the exquisite little book of Ruth—the transcending of national barriers by the love of Naomi and Ruth. But when they deal with Ruth's relationship to Boaz they go completely astray. In the book of Ruth, Boaz marries her because of his strong sense of familial responsibility. But in the movie Ruth and Boaz carry on like a pair of

American young adults trying faithfully to act out the roles Hollywood says young adults must go through. There is instantaneous physical attraction, a little spat, passionate gasping, then a plot obstacle to true love, and then, through a little trick, love conquers the obstacle, and Ruth and Boaz live happily ever after. As Ruth and Boaz are the biblical ancestors of both David and Jesus, there is the suggestion that God's whole plan for history might have been thwarted if Ruth had not made eyes at Boaz.

Love between two people is not something docketed on a relentless pattern of events which begins with catching someone's eye and then ends in physical consummation, or even worse, in a perpetual cycle repeating itself endlessly like a film spliced to itself. For the Christian man, love is that gift bestowed upon people when they engage in common covenant with all the responsibilities and joys attendant thereon. It is not a single emotion that is touched off by a single match which flares and then sputters away. It is friend and companion to suffering and to pain. It is God's greatest gift to his children, elusive, mysterious, and not to be treated like a commodity. It is the very symbol of God's relationship to mankind. It is a gift and neither an achievement nor a magic amulet.

The Christian man doesn't despise the earthy or even the lusty. He sorts out the sick and the neurotic uses of sex and exposes them for what they are. He gives thanks for the faithful response of man to woman and for the family the response creates.

To Be a Man at Worship

- *Is it necessary to participate in worship services in order to be a Christian?*

- *Is it necessarily a good thing to be "spiritual"?*

- *What is the new consensus on worship that is being uncovered in many different branches of the Christian Church?*

- *What is liturgy? Can we get along without it?*

- *What is the true meaning of communion?*

- *In what sense is worship work?*

- *What can we learn when we are lonely before God?*

5

To Be a Man
at Worship

There is a joke that comes out of a seminary class in church administration taken many years ago. It seems that a distinguished foreign visitor was paying a visit to a brand-new church building. The pastor was proudly showing the building to the guest. "Now here is our beautiful new modern kitchen. My, the ladies are proud of that," said the minister. The visitor looked impressed and then said hesitantly, "It is very nice. But, where do you war-shop?" The minister hurried him along and showed him the beautiful new pastor's study replete with oak paneling and a magnificent library. The man looked for a time and said, "It is lovely. But where do you war-shop?" The clergyman hurried him on, pointing out the splendid Sunday school rooms, the church office, the kindergarten, and recreation rooms. Each time the man from abroad expressed appreciation, smiled sadly and asked his persistent question, "Where do you war-shop?" At last, in some impatience, the minister said, "We do have beautiful tile bath rooms and here is one. You can wash up in there."

Now, it certainly is true that we are not careless about appointments for worship in our new churches. Beautiful sanctuaries, windows, carpets, furnishings, and even green planters cover the land. But do we know how to worship as Christians? There seems to be some evidence that we do not. Time and time again, when one gets into a really frank discussion with good active laymen, they confess that they appreciate the purposes of the church but, to be honest, all that liturgy-hymns, scripture, Communion, etc., leaves them cold. They like a good talk by the minister, they say, but the rest they suppose they will have to put up with for the sake of the women and "you ministers," who seem to like that sort of thing.

At the same time there is a genuine hunger for deep religious experience, for the galvanizing of will and emotion, for being caught up out of one's rut and set on a high way.

The major obstacle to worship—the false clue,

it might be called—is the pursuit of the spiritual. Now the life of the spirit is an important New Testament concept. The Holy Spirit touches and enlivens the spirit of man. But the word "spiritual" in our times has drifted from its moorings. It is a conscious synonym for many people with "ideal," "non-physical," "pure," "rarefied." People think this means putting aside the commonplace and pushing consciousness into a state of the contemplation of sterilized goodness. The unspoken synonyms for "spiritual" are often "unreal" and "irrelevant."

This is not the biblical understanding of "spiritual." There, it is more related to life, to the total flesh-and-blood, mind-and-feeling identity that makes you, you and me, me. It is not some ghostly state where you sit with your eyeballs rolled back piously toward the sky.

We have the nineteenth century largely to thank for this "spiritualizing" of religion into sentiment and nostalgia. Worship during that century became subjective, concerned with *my* feelings, *my* motives, and as a psychological preparation for real life. This was true of the revivalist era that left its mark on all of Protestantism and, in a curious way, a wash of a sentimental Bleeding-

Heart-of-Jesus approach in Catholicism. Curiously, the liberal wave within Protestantism did not make much change except to rationalize the assumptions. The old gospel hymn went out, but corporate worship remained a religious program to try to stir people to feel something or do something. Every minister has the experience of leading worship where it is as if the people sit back with arms folded and say silently, "All right, I dare you to excite me, to entertain me, to instruct me. It's up to you. Do it!" It is no wonder that so many men find this an empty experience, curiously unreal and almost zombie-like in quality. There is a mood of mass hypnosis into which many church people enter on Sunday morning at 11 A.M., but it may be a long way from Christian worship.

But there is an encouraging development within Christendom. Twenty years ago William Temple called the ecumenical movement the great new fact of our time. Partly as a by-product of that movement, and partly as a spontaneous experience within many different traditions, there is a growing consensus about Christian worship. This consensus covers developments within Roman Catholicism and some of the most free church traditions. It is not a consensus arrived at by taking a least common denominator approach, but rather one that has sprung from similar conclusions that have been reached independently under the impact of a renewed biblical theology and increased understanding of what worship was like in primitive first-century Christianity. This does not mean that there have been official changes in liturgical rubrics, or broad changes either in Roman or free church parish practice. But within nearly all communions certain front-line groups are proceeding along the same line. The historic chasms of Christendom have not been magically crossed, but there are more hopeful signs of crossing them than there have been for four hundred years.

What are some of the characteristics of this growing consensus? If there is one primary accent, it would be that worship is action, a doing, rather than passive reflection. It centers in the participation of the whole people of God, congregation as well as priest or preacher in liturgical action.

Secondly, this consensus recognizes that there is such a thing as elemental Christian liturgy which is necessary for corporate worship, and that nearly all the present usages have departed from it and are partial expressions of it. This means that the

so-called high church traditions are finding that
they have obscured and disfigured the primary
action of the worshipping community by concen-
trating on unessential embroideries. So-called low
church groups are recognizing that they have re-
placed authentic Christian order with a traditional
programmed order of service which cannot escape
liturgical implications simply because it doesn't
follow a prayer book.

Thirdly, this means a renewed emphasis in all
traditions on the twofold centers of historic Christian worship—first, the reading and expounding
of the scriptures derived from the old synagogue
tradition; and second, the gathering of the people
around the Lord's Table. These are the two feet
on which historic Christian worship rests—the
teaching, preaching, expounding of truth based on
the Bible and the Holy Communion. Only the
Society of Friends historically has departed from
these roots and seemed to remain within the body
of the church, and even there it is because there
is a kind of internalizing of these elements without physical symbol. In this trend advance scouts
in Roman Catholic liturgical renewal emphasize
the place of the Bible and preaching, and Protestants are coming to see the necessity for a sacra-

mental appreciation of the Lord's Supper. These are not planned attempts at correlation worked out by church bureaucrats. These are movements that have grown out of the conviction and experience of radical experimental groups within various churches.

This is really the fourth characteristic—these convictions about liturgy do not come from dabblers in the niceties of correct custom, but from centers in Europe and this continent that are deeply involved in trying to relate the gospel to the modern world.

The Iona Community, begun by George Mac-Leod over twenty years ago, is made up of clergymen and craftsmen under a discipline of witness and worship. The original purpose was to break down the barriers between the church and the common working life of the world. This determination found that it had to come also to a concern for vital worship, as well as a faith that found action in political and social movement. The restored abbey at Iona is a symbol of the dynamic Celtic revival of Christianity in the sixth century, and a hoped-for symbol of a renewed faith in this century.

The Thaize community in France is a brotherhood of Protestants committed to a disciplined and ordered life. Their home base is Thaize, but the brothers work in many different places in the world, in social work, as artists, craftsmen, all under the same discipline. Here, too, there has been a deep concern for a revitalized reformed and catholic worship.

In this country, the Inner City Protestant Parishes have always found that the corporate worship of the parish, gathering around the Table for Communion, and the preaching of the Word, were central to their active participation in the social problems of the slum areas where they carry on their work.

The Christian Faith and Life Community in Austin, starting first with a ministry to students at the University of Texas, and now in a Laos House, carry on their program of theological education for laymen around a center of corporate worship that is not perfunctory exercise but an expression of the very heart of the Community.

These are only a few of perhaps thirty centers where this is happening.

In the light of these two factors, one discouraging and the other encouraging, what is the Christian man doing when he is engaged in the action of worship? First of all, he is stepping into the circle of a transcendent community. That is, he is deliberately placing himself within that mysterious family of relationships that transcends both time and place, bound together by a common loyalty to God revealed in Jesus Christ. Now, this may highlight the reason for the deadness of much of contemporary worship. Many people in our day don't believe that you can be in community with anyone you can't see or who isn't living today. And in addition, there are those who say that their larger community is the whole human race and therefore worship must include little dribs and drabs of representative religious aspirations. There is, of course, no escape from belonging to the whole human race. We are deeply bound to all flesh and blood, but we can be so only intellectually if we are not engaged on a deeper level of our being than simply the fact that we all have skin and the same blood types. Modern man, despite his amazing self-knowledge and incredible facility, tends to become less and less human because he denies his deep instinctual, symbolic needs. We distrust the unknown and try to ignore our mortality. We live only for the present and really believe that history is important only if it provides us with practical lessons for today. All this is foreign to the basic convictions of the Christian faith. Here-and-now and then-and-beyond are all of the same order in God's mind. The Christian faith is filled with myth and symbol. This does not mean that it is archaic or outmoded. God be praised for it, for there is truth that lies below the level of the verbal or the easily articulated. This is not an espousal of a dreamy mysticism. Christianity is not in the main a mystical faith. It is a faith that proclaims that God has built a bridge between eternity and mortality and that bridge is Jesus Christ.

We mean many things when we say that name. We mean a man who really lived and really suffered on a cross. We mean an event in the stream of human history which is an axis on which the whole meaning of human history turns, as far as we are concerned. We mean the continued, active presence of God in the universe and in history. And so Christian worship is the stepping into the whole rich history of meaning that is bound together by Christ. We lift up our hearts in prayer. We hear the special literature of that world read and expounded. We gather around the Table of the Lord, and in an act that is so simple that it is elemental to life itself, we eat and drink. As we do so, we are joined to the whole family of God on earth. How desperately we need to understand and appreciate the sacramental in these times! For so many of us the Lord's Supper has become a time simply of memory and mulling over our problems. Rather it is a very objective act, a glorious festival of celebration when we receive again God's grace and respond with thanksgiving. The Table of the Lord is really the Banquet Table of Heaven around which the whole company of God's people are gathered. We are surrounded by a great cloud of witnesses. All communions are discovering that they have in their precious traditions the belief in the Real Presence of Christ. Too many Protestants have thought that this was just a magical belief of Roman Catholics and they would have none of it. And too many Romans have thought that Protestants had no understanding of the mysterious and awesome power that God has invested in these time-hallowed simple acts. There can be no church without a belief in the Real Presence. Quakers believe in it, as do Romans. Gradually people who have been repulsed and puzzled by awkward superstitions see that the Real Presence is in the gathering of believers around the Table, in the faithful simple acts of the people of God. They come to the Table without rationalization, in simple faith that Christ is really present when his followers name his name and "do this in remembrance of" him.

We do much wistful talking about togetherness and of community. There never can be a deep understanding of what that means until we share deeply in a community of faith, the boundaries of which stretch around the world, back through history, on toward the end of history and into the mysterious reaches of God's own love.

One footnote needs to be added. Such an understanding of transcendent community is not a call to close ranks and begin acting like God's doorkeepers. We do not know these boundaries, and the Fellowship of the Table and the Bible is an open one. God alone keeps the roll books, and our fumbling attempts to take attendance in our religious denominational clubs may be necessary for human engineering but fundamentally they are only tentative lists. Christ is the Only Host at His Table, not the clergyman nor the deacon.

One of the most thrilling services of worship I can remember was at the Inter-Seminary Triennial Conference at Oberlin. There we joined in Christian worship according to the liturgy of the Church of South India. The Church of South

India is a union of Episcopal, Methodist, Presbyterian, and Congregational churches. People who have studied these things believe that this service is the most authentically apostolic extant in Christendom today. It is a full service of prayers, preaching, Offertory, and Communion. There is much participation by the congregation and much sense of movement. This is no passive dull religious show. You have to be with it. At this particular service, presided over by a minister of the Church of South India, the four town churches in Oberlin joined with the students in Finney Chapel. It was a moving occasion, when one sensed the real power of God's church in the world, its vigor, its variety, its beauty, its mystery. It was a real thrill, as a deacon in the service, to help old ladies from the First Congregational Church up the steps, to kneel for the first time in their lives around a table. Their joints were a little rusty, but so were the ears of those from some of the more liturgical traditions a little deafened by the vigorous evangelical preaching of the Word. So Christian worship as we so desperately need it today is stepping into the transcendent community of the Kingdom of God.

Christian worship is the offering up of the

whole of life for scrutiny and blessing. Worship is not escape from the world nor preparation for the real world. It is the most intense kind of work a man can do. Whenever worship gets separated from daily life, then it gets arid and fanciful. This is one of the major marks of Christian worship as distinguished from other religions. There is nothing so material, so common, that God does not touch it with significance. We do need times and occasions when we deliberately offer up our lives and our responsibilities to God as a whole man. We need to look at them in the light of His justice and love; we need to ask his forgiveness for our sins; we need to thank him for his sustaining power and to receive a new assurance of his grace. That is why the Offertory is such an important part of the service, or should be. It belongs closely joined to the Communion service. This is the time when money, as the common symbol of our earthly involvement, is brought to the Holy Table and there placed alongside the common elements of food which have been consecrated as the Holy Elements, and there offered up in thanksgiving. This should be a joyous and incongruous mixture of profane and profound, of sacred and secular.

The Halton parish church, St. Wilfrid's, in Leeds, illustrates this well. Here, Canon Southcott has been at work for fifteen years in an industrial community which, like so many others around the world, gave up much serious interest in church-going half a century ago. Southcott, a passionate man of faith and action, decided that if people wouldn't come to the church the church had to go to them. So every morning of the week the Holy Communion is celebrated on some one's kitchen table at 6 A.M. A few men drop in on their way to work, participate in the sacrament, have a bite of breakfast and then go on to work. In the evening they may gather with their wives in the same house to discuss as a small group what is the message of the gospel for their work or, more particularly, for that street in that community. It is not that this is a pattern to be followed everywhere, but it is a symbol of what must happen—the happy mixture of sacred and secular all across the world's life.

Now in conclusion, having seen worship as joining a transcendent community and as the offering up of the whole of life, let us also see it as the time of true loneliness before God. These are odd times. There are more of us in the world.

We are never out of each other's hair, and yet we are characterized by spells of feeling isolated. We worry terribly about communication. It may be that we need more exposure to a kind of healing loneliness—me, stripped of gadgets and formulae, of plans and diversions, standing before my Creator. Here I face my creatureliness and here only know who God is. This is last on the list because it is the proper order. Individual worship takes its meaning from corporate worship, for the worship of God in Christ is always in communion with the saints. But there are times, and needful ones, often unexpected ones, when we one by one are conscious in new depth of *who* we are and *to whom* we belong.

To be a man—a full man—is to praise God with every fibre of one's being.

A Style, A Cut, A Way of Life

- *Is there such a thing as a Christian personality?*

- *Is it necessary to experience a crisis in one's life in order to have Christian insight?*

- *How can a man walk the razor's edge between a stern self-discipline and a responsiveness to other people?*

- *What is the difference between being human and being natural?*

6

A Style, A Cut,
A Way of Life

There is no greater cliché in liberal Protestantism than the summary of the gospel as "After all, it's a way of life." Often this is said after a particularly hazy discussion about some fine points of doctrine. The way-of-life formula is supposed to brush away as secondary all intellectual considerations about the Christian faith as being fundamentally irrelevant. Such an oversimplification is dangerous.

And yet the Christian faith is an arid philosophy without its anchor in the total personality. It *is* a way of life, not in the sense of being in contradistinction to theology, but in the sense that theology has to find embodiment in order to be Christian. The earliest designation of the Christian people was probably as "followers of the Way."

What does this mean in terms of personality traits? Perhaps nothing has caused more confusion than the attempt to draw psychological portraits of the ideal Christian. Human beings are such elusive creatures. Just when you seem to have a person defined, categorized, identified once and for all, then he does something that seems completely unexplainable. To be meek, compassionate, courageous, persistent, forgiving— all the catalog of virtues that we would like to identify with the Christian man—means to be a bundle of contradictions. When is meekness cowardice, and when is courage obstinacy and egotism? These are the puzzling questions that confront us when we attempt to erect papier-maché dummies of the good man in the display windows of Christendom.

Graham Greene's brilliant novel, *A Burnt Out Case,* reveals some of these difficulties. The main character of the novel is a world-famous architect who retires to a Catholic leper colony in the Congo in his mid-fifties, because he has suddenly faced the barrenness of his life. He finds that he has been fooling himself all his life about both his work and his passionate love affairs. Life holds no meaning for him. The doctor in the colony compares him to a familiar phenomenon in the world of medical treatment for lepers, that is, a person for whom no medicine can arrest the disease until it runs its course, a burnt out case. In spite of himself, the architect gets involved in problems of human misery and performs some acts of real heroism. Everyone proclaims him another Schweitzer, a real saint, despite his desperate denial of any religious faith. What he does, he does almost instinctively.

Another character in the novel is a self-conscious Catholic layman, a self-proclaimed pious man. He says all the right things, but with an empty heart. Greene writes of him that he was "like a wall so plastered over with church announcements that you couldn't even see the brick work behind." In the end his suspicious, super-Christian piety destroys the architect.

It is a very difficult thing to assign traits of Christian character to a man.

Contemporary psychoanalytic understanding has made the task even more difficult. It is now assumed everywhere that the side a person presents to the world is only a small part of his real feelings, and actually what seems to be virtue may hide sin. This is not a new insight. It is as old as the Christian doctrine of man. A superficial understanding of Freud or his descendants can be a dangerous thing. We diagnose people every day as to their real motives, based on little knowledge and much prejudice. On the other hand, we must be grateful to the legitimate practitioners of psychotherapy because they have provided a whole culture with the tools to assess itself on a level other than the superficial. The irresponsible use of this knowledge comes when we make it a weapon to attack people on the basis of partial information. What it ought to do is to make us far more understanding about human weakness and far more appreciative of the capacity for surmounting obstacles that confront everyone.

Every day thousands of people are discredited as being "defensive" or "compulsive" or characterized by some other glib psychological gibe. Daily we consign people into neat little categories that no legitimate psychoanalyst would accept as meaningful for ten seconds. Merely to have learned a new vocabulary for the intricacies of human behavior is worthless. Amateur psychological diagnosis is generally useless if it is not held tentatively, descriptively. It must not take the place of evaluations of people based on the fruits of their labors, the integrity of their word or the genuine limitations under which all men live.

But is there a preferred Christian style of life in terms of temperament? Certainly some eras of Christian history have tended to exalt certain types either subtly or directly as being typically the Christian man. An age of monasticism sees the Christian in terms of the contemplative, the ascetic, the naively innocent. An age of romanticism thinks of the Christian man as the heroic, the courageous follower of the ideal, virile yet chaste. Ages of Protestant vigor have tended to exalt responsibility, balance, commitment without fanaticism.

Now each time, and probably each household on every block, has this much variety contained within itself. There are men of action and there are men of thought. Sometimes there are men who combine with great skill both kinds of traits. There are men of courage who never raise their voices, and there are men of infinite compassion who can never bring themselves to utter words of tenderness. Some have an easily reached sense of humor. Some men are austere and rigid. But none of these traits or combination of traits, pleasant or grating, qualifies a man to wear a tag that marks him as having a Christian personality. The most insidious common assumption is that the friendly, outgoing, gregarious person is a kind of norm for the Christian personality. St. Paul would not have been a good Rotarian, and Martin Luther probably would not have been invited to address the P.T.A. Besides being very satirical, he would have been considered too earthy a speaker for a mixed audience of wholesome American adults.

A Christian temperament is a non-existent entity. Then is one to conclude that the Christian gospel has no reign over the psyche? Is the way of a man's dealing with his fellow men unconditionally set by inheritance and infantile experience? Such a view is a contradiction of the most compelling claims of the gospel itself. In fact, this is the place to begin if we are to know whether Christ's rule over our hearts and minds is to mean anything at all. There are two things that can be explored. First, what the impact of the gospel's claims is supposed to be upon every person, no matter what his personality type. That is, what are the common challenges and dynamics of a life that centers itself on Christ? And second, what are the particularly needful traits of strong Christian conviction in this our time of life and mission? Probably these two questions are best answered together. The eternal claim of Christ upon the individual can never be severed from the stresses of today's peculiar world.

The primary claim of the gospel upon the person is of a *radical awakening*. "Ye must be born again," sounds to many moderns like a sawdust trail, patent medicine appeal to enter a never-never land of religious delusion. And yet this is an essential condition of Christian experience. Some traditions within Christendom would spiritualize this commandment, so that it becomes almost a mystical attribute following inevitably upon the receipt of baptism. The more literal fundamentalist has tended to harden the statement into a fixed emotional pattern. Certain language and certain literal beliefs would thus become a fixed warranty of the legitimacy of the condition.

Both views seem to allow too little freedom and variety of the ways of God with men. Baptism is surely the sign of God's free-given grace, the source of new life with Christ. But men may choose to live fully in that grace or simply ignore what God has given. On the other hand, "to be born again," surely does mean the adoption of a different viewpoint on the meaning of existence, so striking as to approach the dramatic description of rebirth. But to restrict the ways that this may happen and the infinite results that may flow from a man's taking seriously the meaning of God in his life, is to come perilously close to blasphemy.

Another phrase the New Testament uses frequently to describe what happened to people whose lives came in contact with Jesus is, "and their eyes were opened." Surely this characteristic is a necessary part of the life of a mature Christian. At some point, or over a long period of time, a man comes to regard himself and his relationship to the world in a new way. He no longer is propelled by the pressures of his neighbors and his family, or his own inner needs without modification or reflection. From a great sea of impulses, some generous, some fiercely protective of the self, he begins to recognize which are which. This does not mean that he suddenly becomes the complete master of his life, or of himself. It is much more a matter of recognition of who he is, sinner and saint, victim and friend. He begins to make sense out of a great inheritance of doctrine and unspoken feelings about "the world as a whole." He is able perhaps to accept God as more than an interesting abstraction. Things fall into place in some way. His eyes, in effect, are opened. Now this may happen dramatically, or it may take a lifetime. It is never a mechanical process. It is a complex process of self-identification, whereby a man is able to become both more objective and more involved with life at the same time.

Erich Fromm has written about his own psychiatric task:

> Analytic therapy is essentially an attempt to help the patient to gain or regain his capacity for love. If this aim is not fulfilled, nothing but surface changes can be accomplished.[1]

Some such description might also be written of what it means for a man to find the Christian faith as a living factor, rather than just a fact of accidental environment. A man begins to care deeply about his own existence and the meaning of existence. He finds a channel in which these two passions can flow together in the Christian gospel. What seems from the outside a purely

---

[1] Erich Fromm, *Psychoanalysis and Religion* (New Haven: Yale University Press, 1950), p. 87.

personal self-concern and the most abstract question about life become fused together.

Martin Luther agonized in his soul on a quest for personal righteousness. He studied St. Paul's letter to the Romans with the incisive brilliance of a scholarly mind. He also was knocked on his back by a bolt of lightening during a thunderstorm and confessed his utter dependence upon God. These were not separable events for him as far as his religious life was concerned. His mind cried out for answers and his heart bled for something to which he could give himself with complete abandon and passion. "And the just shall live by *faith*," said St. Paul to him directly from the Epistle to the Romans. This meant for him that a whole battery of ideas and convictions were imperative. In the area of doctrine he could no longer accept the intervening work of priest and mass as necessary in the final sense of what must happen for people to be reconciled to God. The great Confessions of Lutheranism and the translation of the Bible into German, so that all men might read directly the Word of God, flowed from this conviction. So also did his decision to leave the life of the celibate and to immerse his life in the common round of events. His whole personality changed from that of being an anxious, un-satisfied man, to a vigorous enjoyer of God's gifts in nature, in love. There was the continual sense that God had won the final victory over sin and death. There were plenty of battles to be fought, no ultimate certainty about intermediate decisions, but there was the ultimate confidence that though the earth shake underneath, God remains a rock. This was both personal and doctrinal.

There are not many Luthers abroad in the land, but this is an almost classic pattern of Christian psychology. Rarely does it happen so dramatically, although in this age of growing despair we should expect to find more dramatic conversions than we do.

If one were to pick out a virtue needed for the Christian life, endurance would be a good one. To stand in the face of the storm, with courage and without panic, is perhaps more a needed ingredient of Christian love than the flash of sympathy. This is not an endurance appropriate to the Stoic. It is not cold and gray, built of despair. It is an endurance that is warmed by the evidence of the mysterious love of God, even in the worst of human situations. More than that, this evidence is taken as token of a final crazy hope that God shall fully reign over his creation.

One of the youthful heroes of two decades ago was a character in Somerset Maugham's novel, *The Razor's Edge*, who was described as loving with a cool passion. In the past decade, the most complimentary remark that teen-agers could make about one another was, "He's cool." There are those who feel that this reflects a detached, cruel attitude toward others. There *is* a kind of "coolness" which reflects a desire to be uninvolved, to enjoy and savor sensation for its own sake, without commitment. (For the bewildered novice in this vocabulary, this is generally referred to as "being hip.")

However, what is implied in the more usual usage of the word cool is being debonair. It means that a person evaluates the situation with insight, with realism, and then hews to a course of his own making insofar as he can. "Loving with a cool passion" may be an overly-romantic notion in the sense that Maugham employed it, but it may be fairly descriptive of the kind of man the times desperately need. We need men who care passionately for the rights of the little guy, for the human instead of the abstract, for the truth as against the public image. But we need men with the discipline of endurance. This discipline has about it then both coolness and passion. This discipline also implies a kind of calculation. There is nothing wrong with taking stock, if the inventory is not weighted with obsessive self-advancement. With the new insights of psychoanalysis it is possible for men to know more surely (and more frighteningly) the inescapable self-interest that is built into every endeavor. But the end use of such knowledge should not be to exploit the sin of selfishness to the hilt. Certain fads of self-interest for the good of all, whether they be in the philosophy of Ayn Rand or a cynical Neo-orthodox distortion of the doctrine of original sin, seem to be trying to do this currently. Christian realism does take stock of the sin of pride and is not shocked to find it everywhere. Christian realism would also require us to repent of it, to subject our free-ranging egoism to the discipline of the two great commandments of the Law.

Men have spent centuries puzzling over the irony of a moral law that demands that we *love* God and *love* others as ourselves. It makes no sense to the casual mind to unite the imperative of "Thou shalt" with the spontaneous, freely given character of human love. The personal pursuit of how to put these two things together is another part of the discipline of endurance. The second birth of New Testament language is in some sense an engagement for the rest of one's life with the puzzle of freedom and law. How can I, daily, respond to others with openness and concern? How do I order my life so I do not become just the puppet of my own guilt feelings or the sinful aggressiveness of others? I must give myself in a great cause, the living out of the will of God's kingdom upon the earth. To that extent I am committed to a calling that is more than my interacting responses to other human beings. At the same time, no other human being can be dealt with as a malleable portion of that calling. Obviously, a man cannot *live* without failing at one point or the other. And that is why the cross has to be encountered somewhere along the road. A man can *die* so that he will fail neither the Kingdom of God's righteousness nor the brother who stands beside him. One did die.

Whatever the temperament of a man, whether he rushes into battles eagerly, or agonizes quietly alone, whether he slips quickly from one ingratiating role to another without knowing it, or stands stolid and lets everyone walk around him, his daily companions are sin and death.

When a man's eyes are opened in the Christian sense, they are in fact opened to recognize both companions. The style of a Christian, then, has to be a daily wrestling with the contradiction of being a sinful child of God while determining and pursuing the use to which a life that will end in death can be put, so that both life and death have meaning.

People will come to different conclusions about the shaping of their life, when their eyes are opened. In that sense every man is cut in his own small image.

Yet we are reminded by the gospel that the way is narrow. It is the puzzling out of the *one* way that God has set out before men in this bewildering age that finds this generation so uncertain. Is the age so corrupt that we must step out of the world in an endless picket line of protest? Or are we called to throw ourselves into the midst of an ambiguous new kind of culture, compromising and fighting? These two different approaches hound us. Which is right?

T. S. Eliot struggled with this very problem in *The Cocktail Party* and could not emerge with

any better answer than there are two ways open
to the Christian in this time. When the eyes of
the leading characters in the play were opened to
themselves and the gospel, two chose to go on
living essentially the same kind of life they had
been leading, but with a new understanding—the
knowledge of their fallibility and of the great
worth of the little battles they wage daily for the
glory of God. One chose to go off to a distant corner of the world and there to give her life up in
heroic martyrdom. Celia, who did this, was the
least likely candidate one could imagine for such
a choice. She was the unencumbered one. Without
hesitation she changed from a straightforward life
of pleasure-seeking to a joy that took death in
its stride.

There are not many such people in this time.
Perhaps not in any time. Filled as we are with
self-analysis and uncertainties about our own
worth, it seems possible for most merely to dig
their feet more squarely into the land where they
find themselves and to await God's leading with
trust. Such a life of human courage tempered
with humor is worthy. God will bless it.

We pray also for the raising up of men who
shudder less at death and who, by the hard un-

conventionality of their martyrdom, will illumi-
nate the path that the rest of us travel.

To be human is not to be natural. To be a man
in the fullest sense is to be disturbed and intrigued
by what we see in Christ.

KANSAS SCHOOL OF RELIGION
University of Kansas
1300 Oread Avenue
LAWRENCE, KANSAS